Chains

The Gospel as It Pertains to Restoration

JESSICA K. JAGER

WESTBOW
PRESS®
A DIVISION OF THOMAS NELSON
& ZONDERVAN

Scripture quotations marked NLT are taken from the Holy Bible, New Living Translation, copyright 1996, 2004, 2007. Used by permission of Tyndale House Publishers, Inc. Carol Stream, Illinois 60188. All rights reserved.

Scripture quotations marked NIV are taken from the Holy Bible, New International Version. NIV. Copyright 1973, 1978, 1984 by International Bible Society. Used by permission of Zondervan. All rights reserved.

Scripture quotations marked MSG are taken from THE MESSAGE. Copyright 1993, 1994, 1995, 1996, 2000, 2001, 2002, 2003 by Eugene H. Peterson. Used by permission of NavPress Publishing Group.

WestBow Press books may be ordered through booksellers or by contacting:

WestBow Press
A Division of Thomas Nelson & Zondervan
1663 Liberty Drive
Bloomington, IN 47403
www.westbowpress.com
1 (866) 928-1240

ISBN: 978-1-5127-7544-0 (sc)
ISBN: 978-1-5127-7546-4 (hc)
ISBN: 978-1-5127-7545-7 (e)

Library of Congress Control Number: 2017902154

Print information available on the last page.

WestBow Press rev. date: 2/27/2017

CONTENTS

Immense in mercy and with an incredible love, he embraced us. He took our sin-dead lives and made us alive in Christ. He did all this on his own, with no help from us! Then he picked us up and set us down in highest heaven in company with Jesus, our Messiah. Now God has us where he wants us, with all the time in this world and the next to shower grace and kindness upon us in Christ Jesus. Saving is all his idea, and all his work. All we do is trust him enough to let him do it. It's God's gift from start to finish!

— *Ephesians 2.5-9, The Message*

"God is aware of your story and names that have come from it ... He is not only aware of them but He is currently and actively redeeming them and recreating them into something that is worthy of display in the palm of His very hand ..."

— *Chains, p.47*

There is no better news than the gospel of Jesus, and no greater freedom than when the Spirit of God takes the good news of the gospel and drives it deep into our hearts. Biblically speaking, the heart is the center of our whole being, the drive shaft of our lives, and the focus of our faith, hope, and love. What we set our hearts on—or what forces its way into our hearts—directs what we think, say, and do. "Above all else," Solomon instructs us, "guard your heart, for everything you do flows from it" (Proverbs 4:23 NIV).

In Luke 4, Jesus takes Isaiah 61:1–2 as his personal mission statement, saying he's come to "bind up the brokenhearted." Jesus came on a mission to make us alive to God again, to restore our hearts, and to makes us into the kind of people who can love God with all our hearts and our neighbors as ourselves. Jesus is on mission to restore our broken, shattered hearts.

But how? How does the good news of Jesus' finished work come into the lives we actually live? How do we connect the shattered parts of our hearts and our stories to the good news of the gospel so that we can begin to experience Jesus' restoration work now?

The beauty of the book you hold in your hands is that it is both an inspiring story of restoration *and* an invitation into your own story of restoration.

Chains is, first of all, the story of someone living now in the process of the healing and restoration of her heart and story.

Jessica Jager is an example of what happens when Jesus comes into a broken heart, into a fragmented story, and begins to heal, renew, and restore. In the following pages, you'll laugh, weep, and rejoice as you read Jessica's story, watching how the resurrected Jesus meets with normal people and does supernatural restoration work. You'll read how Jesus leads us through a very real death on the road to a very real resurrection, training us to renounce what once felt so comfortable in favor of what is actually good and beautiful and real. He has begun a good work in her, and he's bringing it to completion, and you're invited to listen in.

But Chains is emphatically not about Jessica. Jessica's story serves as an invitation to the restoration work Jesus wants to do in you. While it doesn't offer any shortcuts or simple solutions, this book invites you to a very personal journey of restoration and healing. You'll be reminded of the good news of the gospel, the rich resources that are yours in Christ, and the far-reaching implications of all that God has done for you in Christ. You'll be encouraged to know that you are not alone in your sin or shame, that your sisters in Christ are more like you than not, and that you are safe because you are perfectly seen and powerfully loved. And while this book won't "fix" you, it will set you on a trajectory of healing that will shape the rest of your life, helping you have a long-term view of God's sanctifying work in your life, knowing that He's committed to you for the whole process.

And that is the basic roadmap for restoration: Gospel + Safety + Time = Transformation. We're indebted to Ray Ortlund, Jr. for this "transformation equation" that we use in our church all the time and on which Jessica has built this book. What Jessica has done here, though, is a unique and helpful contribution to the current conversation around grace-centered growth and change in the Christian life. While many books talk *about* gospel growth, Chains displays it and invites you into it for yourself.

Jessica is a gift to our church, and the Restore Gatherings (restoregathering.com) she leads have been conduits of restoration for many, many women—in our church and beyond. I'm grateful to be her pastor, grateful that our families get to share life together, and grateful for the ways Jesus is using her in his restoration mission.

As you read, we're asking Jesus to work the full scope of his glorious redemption deep into the broken and shattered places of your story, breaking your chains and setting you free to be who he created you to be.

Steve Hart

EXPLANATION OF RESTORE
AS A MINISTRY

Restore started as a vision for a women's gathering for the purpose of making space for us to dwell in the goodness of the Father as we reflect on the gospel, the safety it offers, and how eternity is our greatest hope. The ministry has been designed to invite renewed awareness of our need for restoration with Him. My heart is for women to experience renewed belief in Him, as well as knowledge of the greatest rescue plan ever written—and for them to ultimately know it was written for them. That rescue plan wasn't just meant for those who appear to have it all together but for those empowered by the gospel to lay themselves at the foot of the cross, praying to be cut free. God sees our chains. He knows how they got there, how we put them on, who put them on—and He has a plan to cut them and set us free.

What if your story didn't just include hurt but included a story of pursuit and ultimate rescue? What if you could share that story freely without shame or fear of where you've been? What if you primarily felt the hope of where you are headed—through His power, not your own—through His love for you, through His knowledge of you, through His constant and active care cultivating all of the yuck and all of the joy? What if you could experience the intertwining of it all in a way that allowed you to see the promise of heaven in every corner? I know it to be His heart, and I know it to be His will.

Because of my awareness of our need for restoration with Him, I am praying for women to be freed from the chains that bind their hearts and to be aware of the gospel in a way that allows them to find their safety in Him, which will also allow them to gather and rejoice in those above-mentioned truths, ultimately becoming aware of the freedom that is offered to us through what Jesus has done for each of us separately and all of us collectively. This single prayer is so heavy on my heart that I can not possibly bear it alone anymore. Please join me in it. God has a desire for us all to experience deep community with one another, and I do not believe for a second that women are being left out of this desire. What if we knew we were protected and loved enough that we could freely confess our mess to one another? And what if those around us were aware enough of that same truth to wrap us up in it rather than in condemnation? What if when we saw each other's chains we felt no shame or judgment? What if we desired to draw nearer to one another in order for those chains to break as we reminded each other of the goodness we have been given to claim in Him?

Restoration is continual. We will never stop needing it. We will never get to a place where we will have figured it out. And with that knowledge we are given great hope that He will never revoke our invitation nor forsake us in our need. I realize that this message involves risk, that it involves vulnerability and an invitation to let go of some things that probably feel quite safe. I have not been left out of those experiences; He has been good to show me some pretty dark and dusty corners of my own heart through this last year, allowing me to be the ultimate guinea pig in a lot of this. And I can testify to His existence and constant availability to supply me with His mercy and His grace. Still, I realize that this may not sound like good news to some of you. Please know that there is grace enough for you. We serve a patient and kind Father as daughters of a king who has not come to burn us but to raise us up. This process takes time, which has been made available to us through that blood of His son. We are safe to come and listen and rest in in the truth and be honest about where we are in our stories. We are loved and known and seen and delighted in already, and we will continue to be so. This rest and safety will be our constant prayer and the purpose of all that we enter into with Him.

CHAPTER 1

CHAINS

So we have stopped evaluating others from a human point of view. At one time we thought of Christ merely from a human point of view. How differently we see him now! This means that anyone who belongs to Christ has become a new person. The old life is gone and a new life has begun! And all of this is a gift from God, who brought us back to Himself through Christ. And God has given us a task of reconciling people to Him. For God was in Christ reconciling the world to Himself no longer counting people's sins against them. And He gave us this wonderful message of reconciliation.

—2 Corinthians 5:16–19 NLT

I think it is important to understand where our need for personal restoration with Jesus comes from. I have taken the liberty of describing our need with the metaphor of chains.

Our chains are the things that keep us from experiencing the goodness that God intended for us through the sacrifice of Jesus. They are the things that we accept instead of the freedom that has been offered. They all look different and behave differently. Some are removable or are activated less often, whereas others act as a filter for how we relate to the majority of the experiences we encounter. Yet they all come from a need to self-protect from someone or something—through them we meet our need to be hidden and to be unknown or support the feeling of being unknown. These chains can be the belief that we are too much or not enough—our understanding of our worthiness or our desire to prove. Maybe you feel unheard, or maybe you relate as an orphan, a widow, or the like—operating out of the belief that you have been abandoned. Perhaps you feel unlovable or unwanted, and maybe you feel a need to have it all together, to look good, or to be perfect.

As you begin to listen for others' chains and hear where they are rooted and what they are rooted in, I want you to recognize that although some stories may be more dramatic, more shocking, or more weighty than others, this does not change the amount of destruction they cause in our relationships with Jesus. They all look different, but they all hold equal strength and equal pain. And they are all still met with the same invitation of promise, hope, and truth that comes with the freedom we have been given in Jesus. And through that knowledge we are more alike than different.

Some of you may have difficulty determining what your chains are, let alone giving them names. I have already prayed for those of you. Please do not let the realization separate you or make you feel unworthy or inept. Please share your feelings with someone you trust and ask him or her to walk through this with you so that you can be wrapped up in His love and so you can be made aware of your need. Your story is worthy and worth sorting through, and your heart is worthy of pursuit.

There are three questions that are helpful when mapping out your chains.

1. **What are my chains?**

2. **Where did they come from, or potentially, who gave them to me?**

3. **How do they manifest themselves or cause me to relate in my relationships with Jesus and others?**

My chains are intertwined with the themes of self-reliance, a need to prove independence, and an inability to trust, rely on, or depend on anyone without feeling as if I am a burden. I have had a hard time marking myself as lovable or worthy of love, believing most often that love was meant for me to pour out but not receive.

These chains came from a childhood of not knowing exactly what to expect. Years of ignored trauma and circumstance led to the creation of my chains. At times the chains have even served as a means of survival, as trusting others or putting my hope in the care of others would have not only been risky but also surely ended up in failure or pain.

These chains have manifested themselves in many ways, and they most commonly play out in a need to do everything myself. I have a need to prove that I can do anything, and I go through life as if I have an inability to fail. If any of this is threatened or judged, I become defensive. God, through Jesus, has slowly been dealing with these chains, but they still show up—and more often than I would like. Recently, a friend who knew about my body and its ailments insisted on carrying a box that I felt the need to carry myself; I knew I could carry it, and I felt weak allowing her to do it. But on the flip side, coming alongside me and physically doing something for me is one of the most tender ways she can love me and show me care. My response was a growl, and my friend asked, *Did you just growl at me?* My response was, *Sure did!* I let her carry the box, but the growl had come out of my inner groaning—it was an audible sign of my humanness and its need for the ultimate healing that will only come with the return of Jesus. This restoration process will be continual. That knowledge comes with comfort and, at times, resentment as the waiting draws out an impatience that He is able to turn into humble longing. At times these patterns of relating have made me unsafe to love, unsafe to touch, and unsafe to move toward. My chains have affected relations with my husband, girlfriends, children, and extended family as I have fought to hold on to them rather than be set free. They have impeded my growth, deepened my wounds, and kept me from experiencing the fullness of His love for me. But through the vulnerability that has been made available to me through Him and what He has done, He is healing even my desire to cling to my chains as He makes room for me to ask for forgiveness, confess my need, and explain my chains. Through that He sets me all the more free.

Each chapter in this book will hold personal stories of my relating to each of these themes. I find it important to point out that these experiences are told from my side of the story—out of the realization of my need and the knowledge of how Jesus has worked through them out of His goodness, grace, and mercy. These stories involve others who have been connected to them and have a place within the story, but God has done much work to provide for me in each story so that I don't need all relationships to be a certain way or others to act or behave in a certain way; He has done so to redeem and restore my heart. I have learned that His grace is not only sufficient for those around me but for me as well—and that has been a gift, friends.

This story holds much shame and brokenness as well as risk, hiding, and confession. This confession has included an unmasking of my shame and an emergence from the safety of my hiding, and it has involved the one person on this earth whom I trust with all my heart—my husband.

Brian and I were married when I was nineteen, and this was a time when my chains were most visible to me. I had every intention of making them stronger, and self-protection and proving became close friends of mine—and being known was even more risky. I had never experienced real love before this point—not the kind that seemed to know me and love me anyway, and not the kind that was promised to me unconditionally. One would think that in light of this reality my marriage would come as a great source of healing; however, because of the condition and ramifications of my chains, I was not able to experience healing in Brian's love for me. Rather, it just was all the more justification for me to further my need for self-reliance, proving myself, and independence. I felt the love, and it was overwhelming. But instead of allowing it to fan my flame, I let it crush me. And through the fear of not wanting to lose that love, I lengthened my chains, believing that there was much I could do to threaten Brian's love for me but not much I could do to grow it. So started fourteen years of hiding my need, taking care of myself, defusing our problems, and taking on the weight of potential problems before they even started.

About four months into our marriage, I became pregnant. We didn't believe that I could become pregnant due to some health complications in my past, so we had not been actively trying to prevent pregnancy. After thinking I had contracted the worst version of the flu for about two weeks, my mom gently reminded me that married ladies get pregnant. You would think that this would cause elation—and in many ways it did—but it was also met with great fear; I knew that if we had been planning this, I would not have become pregnant in this time.

And so ensued another week of hiding until I finally told Brian that we may be expecting a little one—a miracle that we wouldn't be able to comprehend the depths of until the day of our son's birth when we would look back and reflect on all that had taken place between the day I found out I was with child to the day he was born. Brian's reaction to the news was one that had the power to heal, but I met it with a greater need to hide, to suck it up and deal, and to pull up my bootstraps to care for myself and to make sure I did not inconvenience or burden him. He was full of joy, free from fear, and overwhelmed with excitement as he called me at least five times on the way home to see if I had taken a test yet to confirm our suspicions.

We were pregnant. All I had ever wanted was to be a mom, and in many ways Elliot will always signify a dream come true for me. But what lay in the in between was nine months of all-day sickness—if I was awake, I was throwing up—doctor and hospital visits, rehydration treatments, efforts to stop labor, lots of monitoring, twenty weeks of preterm labor and bed rest, more appointments, and more fear. I had complicated migraines that presented themselves as strokes, including blindness and loss of speech.

Again, one would think this would have bound us together, and in some ways it did. But mostly, this reaffirmed my need to hide, to take care of myself, and to carry the burden so Brian could continue doing what he needed to do; it reaffirmed my need to pull up my bootstraps and minimize my need and the severity of the situation. At this time, I had written in my journal that good wives don't let their babies die and begged the Lord to allow me to do what was necessary to keep that from happening, to make sure this baby was born healthy and safe. It was deep, it was on me, and I had the potential to ruin everything. My body's inability to deal, to provide safe harbor for this growing life was my fault, my weakness, and my burden.

And so it continued throughout the journey of this pregnancy. My job became predicting my sickness, being able to drive myself to appointments, check myself into the hospital, and drive myself home. By the time Elliot was born we had sixteen hospital visits and thirty doctor appointments and I had only asked Brian to accompany me four times—two hospital visits, one ultrasound, and the birth of our tiny miracle. Being in the shackled state I was in, and not knowing the ramifications of my chains, I had set us up from the beginning with our own form of normal relating: two separate entities headed toward the same goal but in our own lanes, only crossing over when I could let down my guard, which required complete incapacitation, lack of consciousness or complete inability.

The years that followed would be consistent in pattern: we would have another viable pregnancy two years later that was nearly identical, but we were doing it with a toddler in tow. It still didn't break me, but boy did it wound my heart. The deeper we got, the more I would blame and resent Brian for what was taking place. I made him out to be a deserter when things got rough. I told myself and believed lies that he didn't and wouldn't care, and I bathed in the lie that it was my fault because I was and always had been too much to handle. Sure, he could have made different choices; he could have moved toward me, but that would have been risky and potentially could have broken us, because I would have seen his pursuit as judgment, as his realization that I couldn't handle what I had been given—and so we continued.

In more recent years God has worked on my heart in relation to Himself. I have slowly handed Him links of my chains, entire lengths of chains, and I have watched Him break them, and at times burn them. As a result of those times, I became quite discontent with the state of our marriage.

Two years ago, I came to a crossroads. We were at the most stressful and broken part of our loving one another. Brian was at a tense and stressful point professionally; I had given him false freedom to choose what he thought was best for us, and he was feeling the weight of having to choose rightly. We were being pulled apart. *I love you* was lost and defensive attack and protection were prevalent. I was incredibly unable and unwilling to love him where he was at and was actively praying for God to change him. Through this prayer, I nearly audibly heard the Spirit speak to me, saying, *you're either going to love him or you're not.* This revelation caused me to fall on my face in repentance; I had been praying for my husband to change for my comfort, not his redemption, praying for him to see my need so I didn't have to ask God to meet it. I had expected Brian to hold it all together and keep me happy because it was risky to ask God to do it. I knew relying on God would require me to let go of some things. And through the next days, weeks, and months, my need for my husband's perfection was replaced with the knowledge of God's.

This past January the Spirit moved freshly in this wound. He gave me another opportunity to choose healing. Once again, He brought my unbelief to the surface, and I realized that I had given power to my husband that he had no ability to hold. And in doing so, my chains had become mine alone to heal. I came to understand that I had been believing that not even God would be enough to heal me, hold me, or love me. I was, in my mind, unlovable, and not even the love of that Father would be enough to prove otherwise. This unbelief was gross to me; it was disgusting and vile, and it made me want to run. Self-loathing threatened and shame knocked at the door, but the Spirit showed me something different. **I could confess, even to others, because I was known, loved, and pursued— even in and through this. God delighted in me enough to speak and lead me into a different reality, where I could experience what had actually been intended for me from the beginning: undying, unconditional, patient, eternal, never-ending, everlasting, constant, steadfast love!**

So I sat face to face with Brian, and I said, *I have to confess to you and ask you to forgive me for chaining myself to you. I have to confess to you the role that I have played in how you relate to me, which is how I have asked you to.* His question that followed was one that would have had potential to further chain me, to cause me to live like the prisoner I believed I was, if I had entered in without the power of cross behind me, without the everlasting truth of the gospel. *How long has this been going on?* I answered, *Fourteen years, every moment we have spent together, every time I have said I love you, or made a mistake, through the birth of our children, through sickness and health—it is in every corner, and I'm sorry.* His reply was one that I will never forget, *That's not marriage, babe, and I'm so sorry that's what it's been.*

We weeped and we prayed. It took fourteen years to be freed, and it could take another fourteen years to heal. But through this I experienced an unshackling, and through that unshackling I was given opportunity to believe in the gospel and my identity in it. I trusted in the safety of His knowledge of my sin and shame and His delight in me—and the realization that this wouldn't be fixed overnight and it didn't need to be.

2 Corinthians 5:16–19 reminds us what it means to belong to Christ—We are new in and through Him, restoration is a gift He determined me worthy to receive, and through it I am continually reconciled to Him. My sins are no longer numbered but thoroughly and forever wiped and washed clean. And He left me not only with His word for my ultimate guide but His very Spirit.

The gift of restoration is not earned through our own ability to be good, our availability, our knowledge, our strength, nor even our belief. It has been made available and been carried out through the flow and power of the blood that He so graciously and mercifully gave for each of us. Live in that, friends. Be loved in that, friends, because that truth has the power to cut you free—to break and burn your chains forevermore.

Reading through Paul's letters, I am easily gripped by his heart for others to know Jesus and to live in awareness of the gospel. In 2 Timothy, it is humbling to know that Paul was in prison. He had been chained and abandoned by almost all who knew him, and yet he was still preaching, still encouraging, still empowering, still loving those he felt called to serve. We know that during this time it was extremely dangerous to reveal or claim faith in Christ outwardly in Rome. It could have proven fatal or landed them in jail like Paul. And so what happened with Paul was complete desertion due to his chains by all except for one.

> **As you know, everyone from the province of Asia has deserted me—even Phygelus and Hermogenes. May the Lord show special kindness to Onesiphorus and all his family because he often visited and encouraged me. He was never ashamed of me because I was in chains.**
>
> **—2 Timothy 1:15–16 NLT**

These verses struck me in two ways:

1. **Onesiphorus was able to rest in the safety of God's love for him to not fear the repercussions of being associated with Paul, a chained, jailed proclaimer of Christ. He risked it all to love his brother: his reputation, his family, his life, all to reach out and say, *I see you and you are loved.***

2. **Paul was chained, but he was free. With his chains he was bound to his location, but they could not bind him from his belief or his ability to speak. For he knew Jesus**

had in fact died for him and the chains were a part of the very story set for him. And in that, he flourished.

Most of our chains are not physical, but they are no less powerful in the lies they tell us about what we can and cannot do, how we can or cannot be loved by or love others, how we can or cannot participate in community with others. Jesus died to free us from being bound by them. They may be present, and it may take us until we reach the gates of heaven to be completely released, but we are still free, my friends. Jesus died as an act of love and mercy for our souls. That gift is for now—not later when we are good, or healed from sickness, or different, or completely changed. We are free from all of those things by His righteousness. Not by our will but through His sacrifice. It is finished.

God has a desire for us all to experience a deep communion with one another, and I do not believe for a second that women are being left out of this desire. What if we knew we were protected and loved enough that we could freely confess our mess to one another? And what if those of us listening were aware enough of that same truth to wrap the other up in freedom and truth rather than condemnation? What if when we saw each other's chains we felt no shame or judgement but we desired to draw more near to one another in order for them to break as we reminded each other of the goodness we have been given to claim in Him?

We are not left to our own devices. We are not alone, and we are not our own. We belong to a mighty king who has marked us all as daughters, which links us together in a sisterhood.

It is my hope that you will take time to dig into these themes with some other ladies. With friends who can hold your heart and hear your story in light of who He is and what He's done— and in light of what that says about your identity and who you are when found in the light of His face, which shines upon you in delight.

Your story is worthy and worth sorting through, and your heart is worth pursuit. Use these questions as a way to share your hearts and story with one another.

1. **What are your chains?**

2. **Where did they come from or who gave them to you?**

3. **How have they and how do they manifest themselves in your relationship with Jesus and with others?**

Use this time to wrap each other in truth and love as you look for ways to cover those chains in His love and His view of you. Work toward seeing and searching out the heart instead of behavior as you listen.

We Are Not Left To Our Own Devices.

We Are Not Alone.

We Are Not Our Own.

We belong to a mighty king who has marked us as daughters—as we seek out restoration with Him, we will also be freed into a relationship of sisterhood with one another.

CHAINS

CHAINS

_____
_____
_____
_____
_____
_____
_____
_____
_____
_____
_____
_____
_____
_____
_____
_____
_____
_____
_____
_____
_____
_____
_____
_____
_____
_____
_____
_____
_____
_____
_____

CHAINS

CHAPTER 2

GOSPEL

You know what I was like when I followed the Jewish religion—how I violently persecuted God's church. I did my best to destroy it. I was far ahead of my fellow Jews in my zeal for the traditions of my ancestors. But even before I was born, God chose me and called me by His marvelous grace. Then it pleased Him to reveal His Son to me so that I would proclaim the Good News about Jesus to the Gentiles.

— Galatians 1:13–16 NLT

A big piece of restoration is the concept of story: we each have one, and God is moving and pursuing each of us through our stories in a way that is personal to who we are in Him. The gospel is the good news of our freedom and its effect on our identities. We were determined worthy of a sacrifice before we were even born, and His love came to break us free from our chains. His sacrifice reminds us that He lived the perfect life so we wouldn't have to and that his life was made as a substitute for ours on the cross. Our need is not only welcome but necessary—we were designed to need Him, and to require His fellowship. Through this, we have been given the privilege of repentance and confession, which is meant to remove us from our shameful state and restore us as a beloved to Him.

This gives us a fourth question:

• **What do you need to believe about the work of Jesus and what it declares about you in Him to be set free, to have your chains broken and burned?**

I need to believe that it is personal, and that Jesus died for me, that He is my Jesus. That He not only died because of me but also for me. Because of my chains, I have had great difficulty in seeing that Jesus died specifically for me as much as He has for everyone else. Because of my chains, I often have added on the formalities of extra law and a need for penance for my failure or shortcomings. Worth through works became a comfortable arrangement for me. I could earn my way to heaven. I could prove myself worthy of the Kingdom. I believed I needed to make myself worthy of the sacrifice that had already been made with me in mind. I was living in a state of unfinished work. I was living in a state of belief that I held a piece of the work that needed to be finished. And even though I felt like a failure, I would keep working because the work was my only hope.

Many of my chains are wrapped in the fear of being known, fully known, faults and failures, past and present. They are wrapped in the fear that the shame of my upbringing and the shame that comes out of my reaction to it would become known. As a little girl, one of my earliest memories took place when I was about four years old. I had gotten in trouble one morning, as I had been found under our table cradling our milk. We didn't have much food to speak of, money was always tight, and now I had spoiled the milk by keeping it out all night. How would we afford more? The reason I had fallen asleep there was because I had actually gotten the milk out to try to feed my hungry baby sister in the middle of the night—something I had done dozens of times before—but the carton was too full for me to fill her bottle without spilling, so I fell asleep trying. I have countless stories that reflect these same tendencies: me trying to care for those around me but being limited in my success due to my size and age, not my heart.

I came to know Jesus my sophomore year of high school. I interpreted my role as living out a life in Christ through works and being good. Having my background and my upbringing, this was good news to me. My whole life I had been good and worked hard, and that had never been enough for my parents. But in my interpretation that was what God wanted, and it would be enough. This turned into years of service, covering works with the description of calling. Simply because someone had asked me to do something and I could succeed in fulfilling their wishes, this was Kingdom work. Youth Group leadership, worship team, and children's church were all part of a calling I had to serve, and each task I completed was insurance for my entrance to heaven. But each failing was something I would need to do penance for. Earn, fail, earn some more.

This pattern translated into my adult life in various ways—earning turned into striving. Striving to be the best, to never fail anyone, to get stuff done. And most of the time I was successful, which was a nail in my own coffin, because when I couldn't meet needs, when I felt like I couldn't possibly move forward or do it all or take on more responsibility, I felt like a failure—when really I was just human. Being the best meant having lists of things that I needed to complete. Being the best mom meant feeding my children the right food, volunteering my soul to their school—every field trip, every assembly—baking fresh cookies everyday after school, tucking them in with stories and prayers every night, and getting them to the point where they would ask Jesus into their hearts by age five. That's what success would look like; that's what doing my job as a Christian mom would look like. I also had a list for being a good wife: look nice, be fit, cook, entertain, date, have sex as often as possible, be flexible, hold the peace in our home, make sure Brian can go to work and come home without any stress on him, take weekends away, help provide, and do it all. Each of my other hats had a similar list, and when the lists went unfulfilled, boxes unchecked, I was the one who needed to clean it up and then come to the Father and repent, begging for restoration, begging for forgiveness and another chance at the Kingdom. It was exhausting and truly lonely.

Before we moved to Spokane, I was classroom mom, president of the school's fundraising committee, head of children's church, worship leader, owner of a very successful catering business, teacher three days a week at our local homeschool co-op. I was also working out three days a week at 5:15, because that was the only time I could get it done, and running 20–30 miles per week. This was on top of all of the normal responsibilities I had as a mom and a wife. Most nights I would fall asleep begging and pleading with God to give me another shot, confessing that I had fallen short, that I could have done more and if He would just give me one more chance at the Kingdom I would do better the next day. I was in fact my own Jesus, living outside the freedom of the cross and continually binding myself more tightly in my chains. I was the only one who could keep the schedule, care for my kids, love my husband, feed us, provide for us, and ultimately, I was the only one who could save us.

When we moved to Spokane, my list of things to do disappeared, as there was, in my mind, nothing that I could do that would be of value. We lived in a nearly 5,000-square-foot house, and so my new mission and way to prove my worth and value was making sure that thing was spotless. But that was all. No one needed me, and the one thing I was needed for was not worthy in my eyes. What do you mean *just be a mom*? What do you mean *just be a wife*? I can do that with my eyes closed. What else? I believe God used that time as a stripping of sorts, I was left with nothing to cling to, hide in, or gain value from. That would change.

About 6 months later we started to attend church gatherings at Soma. My ears allowed me to hear the gospel for the first time, and I was ticked. Who was this preacher man offering us freedom and not giving us anything to do? When was He going to tell us how unworthy we were or what to do next to make it better? And who was this Jesus he spoke of? It took about three months until the gospel broke me. This started a year of not being able to enter the building without weeping. No one would even have to preach or sing a word, and I would be in full tears. Each week the Spirit would wash over me anew, gently showing me that I was this sinner they sang of and spoke of, but I was free to repent, receive grace, and move forward knowing that I had been forgiven, free from shame.

What became apparent is that I had known nothing of the gospel, and I mourned the loss of the years that I had lived outside of it. I had known nothing of a savior who died so that I could live in freedom. I believed everyone to be worthy of that but me. It had never been personal, and it had held no power for me. I had no knowledge of the safety of the everlasting forgiveness that came out of Christ's finished work. God had created me in His own image, and I had been living under the weight of knowing that I was responsible for breaking that. But I had left out the story of redemption and grace, leaving out the truth that I was ultimately forgiven—it was and is finished forever and ever. In that unbelief, I was still dead, unable to experience the fullness of the gift that had been offered to me because each of my chains held a reason why I couldn't accept the gift. And each chain held a belief that even if I did give Him my chains, I would be turned away. And each chain showed me that I still had work to do.

> You know what I was like when I followed the Jewish religion—how I violently persecuted God's church. I did my best to destroy it. I was far ahead of my fellow Jews in my zeal for the traditions of my ancestors. But even before I was born, God chose me and called me by His marvelous grace. Then it pleased Him to reveal His Son to me so that I would proclaim the Good News about Jesus to the Gentiles.
>
> —Galatians 1:13–16 NLT

What I needed to believe was that the gospel was bigger than my fear and despair. What I needed to believe was that Jesus died for me personally, for my need and sin and shame. I needed to believe that repentance was a gift, not intended to make me experience further shame—that the act of confession would be a practice and reminder of my freeing, that it was a part of my restoration and not meant to set me even farther apart from Him. What I needed to know was that He was aware of my past yet still had a future for me—I was not a liability to the plan. Coming to this realization allowed me to see myself as a daughter of a high king who had determined that I was worthy of rescue, love, and care. It allowed me to see not only that my sin required the death of my savior but also that by His death I was determined worthy of an invitation to a new life. There were a few things that I had been taught through the actions and experiences of my childhood: trust was not an option, faith in being cared for was dangerous, and forgiveness was never offered. In some way, this broke my faith in Christ before it even began. The gospel tells me that Christ lived a perfect life in my place, died a death as a substitute for me on the cross, rose from the grave to begin a new creation on earth, and then ultimately ascended to heaven. He did not leave us alone, though, but left us with His Spirit so that we would never be without Him as we wait for His return. This leaves me with some healing and restorative truths for my personal story, but they are just as true for you.

- We are free to repent, because forgiveness has already been given. We can mourn our sin, but ultimately we are welcomed and free to turn from it and instead turn toward the Kingdom.

- We can have faith through the knowledge of what He has already done and what He intends to do, trusting in Christ for our salvation, finally letting go of our own need to save ourselves, allowing us to rest and receive.

- God has not only blotted out our sin but removed it. In doing so, He has reconciled and restored us to Himself, allowing us to approach the throne enveloped in His righteousness, clean and white as snow. And in doing so, He has made us eternally right with Himself.

- In the moment we first believed, He traded His righteousness for our sins. That is an external symbol of His kindness—trading something of absolute and infinite value for something that is worthless.

- We can trust that we are no longer His enemy—rather we are His children, and through that we have been given the privilege of encouraging others to see Him has Father as well.

Not only are these truths healing but also because of them we are forever changed—unchained and handed the keys of the Kingdom. With those keys, we are given not only access to the Kingdom but also privilege to share them with others.

This gospel, this truth and freedom, is a gift, and with that gift comes a choice to show Him your chains, knowing full well that He already sees them and desires nothing more than for you to be set free. Sharing our chains with God has the power to turn us into a people who proclaim His grace, of which we are not only so unaware but also so desperately in need, which has been made available to us through the blood of Jesus. This grace allows us not only to experience the gospel and Jesus fully but also to reach out and share it with those around us without the fear of having to save anyone but instead with love. Jesus will do the saving. Through this grace we are given a calling to be a community that not only proclaims but also embodies this truth. We are able to become a transformed body of believers and a family wrapped in true hope and the knowledge of His strength to fulfill that hope. This is the outpouring of restored relationship with Him. We become that community through holding tightly to the truth, and through being ultimately true to one another. We become that community through acknowledging His authority over us and obeying the gospel, which means living according to these truths: that God created the world, sent His son to save it through His death and suffering in our place, rose from the dead, and ascended to His rightful place—not leaving us alone but with His very Spirit and His power. And through all of that we are welcomed to simply repent and trust in Christ for our forgiveness.

A big piece of our experience of restoration is the telling of our stories.

Everyone has a story, and God is moving and pursuing you through yours in a way that is personal to who you are in Him. Sifting through the highlights and lowlights of your story will help you see where you have seen Him and where you long for Him to be.

This question proves quite helpful for that purpose.

• **What does the good work of Jesus declare about me? And how has it come to set me free?**

Your need is not only welcome but necessary—you were designed to need him. This may require not only confession but also repentance, which was provided for you through His sacrifice, which is meant to remove you from your shameful state and restore you as beloved to Him. The gospel is a gift that comes with an opportunity to hand Him your chains, fully knowing that He already sees them and desires nothing more than for you to be set free.

CHAINS

_____

_____

_____

_____

_____

_____

_____

_____

_____

_____

_____

_____

_____

_____

_____

_____

_____

_____

_____

_____

_____

_____

_____

_____

_____

_____

_____

_____

Chapter 3

SAFETY

We are safe because we are named by Him and His righteousness. He knows us in terms of our story—not only its beginning but also its current status and its end, when we will have fully taken on the righteousness of Christ.

> Lord, you have examined my heart
> and know everything about me.
> You know when I sit down or stand up.
> You know my thoughts even when I'm far away.
> You see me when I travel
> and when I rest at home.
> You know everything I do.
> You know what I am going to say
> even before I say it, Lord.
> You go before me and follow me.
> You place your hand of blessing on my head.
> Such knowledge is too wonderful for me,
> too great for me to understand!
> I can never escape from your Spirit!

I can never get away from your presence!
If I go up to heaven, you are there;
if I go down to the grave, you are there.
If I ride the wings of the morning,
if I dwell by the farthest oceans,
even there your hand will guide me,
and your strength will support me.
I could ask the darkness to hide me
and the light around me to become night—
but even in darkness I cannot hide from you.
To you the night shines as bright as day.
Darkness and light are the same to you.
You made all the delicate, inner parts of my body
and knit me together in my mother's womb.
Thank you for making me so wonderfully complex!
Your workmanship is marvelous—how well I
know it.
You watched me as I was being formed in utter
seclusion,
as I was woven together in the dark of the womb.
You saw me before I was born.
Every day of my life was recorded in your book.
Every moment was laid out
before a single day had passed.
How precious are your thoughts about me, O God.
They cannot be numbered!
I can't even count them;

they outnumber the grains of sand!
And when I wake up,
you are still with me!

—Psalm 139: 1–18 NLT

I have stories I would rather hold in, experiences that bring me great shame. Stories that I believe confirm the very most awful things I believe to be true about myself—even if just on a subconscious level. And out of those stories have come names, names and descriptions that I would rather not have others know. I fear that those names would encourage others to see those things in me, too, or even reveal what is actually true about me.

We all have these names, we all have these hurts and wounds—some self-inflicted, some provided by others. But they exist nonetheless. They make us feel unsafe. They make us feel unknown. They cause us to hide and to create space and distance. They hold us back from experiencing community in the way Jesus made possible through his sacrifice for us. They keep us from sharing in the trueness of our creation and the goodness of our Father. They create patterns of relating and "truths" that do not reflect the Kingdom, yet we find comfort in them as well.

Perhaps the names you have are self-given. Perhaps they are connected to your outward appearance: skinny, fat, tall, short, curvy, weak, fit, broken. Perhaps some of these even feel good to have related to you; perhaps they are names that give you strength or good standing. Perhaps you have names given to you by and through the way you relate with others: capable, incapable, flaky, late, unreliable, insensitive, selfish, unkind, dramatic. Perhaps there are names that come from wounding: unworthy, unneeded, unwanted, too much, not enough, abandoned, orphaned, widowed, or the like.

- I want to encourage you to take a quick inventory of your names.

- I want you to take a few moments to organize them.

- I want you to think for a moment how willing you would be to speak them out loud.

- If you are now laughing or sweating, I want to know why.

Even now, as I type and prepare these words, I find myself pulling into my shell, almost arguing with the Spirit about what He has prepared for me to share, because being hidden has it perks and involves what at least seems like a whole lot less risk.

As a little girl, I had responsibilities that stacked higher than my actual standing. I had parents who were incapable of caring for me. I spent most of the first twenty years of my life sometimes feeling and most of the time knowing that I was too much, that I was a burden. I knew from a young age that I had a role as savior, that I had a role as fixer and doer, that I had a role of being safety for others, that I had the role of taking blows so others could remain upright. Some of the names I picked up from those first two decades were sensitive, dramatic, pretty, abandoned, unwanted, unworthy, orphan, too much. There are multiple stories for each one.

There was a period of time when I was left in the care of my father without the presence of my mother. That was a pivotal year and half for me. I was six years old, and sleeping had never felt safe—there was a lot that could happen while I slept. My sister could wake and need me. I could wake up to the sounds of shouting and screaming. I could wake to the absence of my dad and the weary shell of my mother. Sleeping was risky. And over that year and a half I stopped sleeping altogether. I would crawl into my sister's bed every night and hold her tightly and whisper the words *I love you* until she fell asleep. And then I would lay awake making sure nothing would come for us in the night. Some nights my dad would leave and not return until the wee hours. On those nights, I would put myself to bed, check all the windows and doors, and sit next to the door of our bedroom making sure nothing would come through without passing me first. During school hours, I would worry for my family, and I would worry for what the night would hold.

One night we went to the playground at the school down the street. My dad walked us down, and as I was playing, I fell from the bars mid penny drop. As I fell, the name of the Lord slipped from my lips. At the time they were merely words I had heard another kid at school say, and as your average six year old will do, I gave them a whirl. I was not raised in a Christian home; as I grew, my mother explained to me that religion was private and personal and left to each person's heart to decide what was best for him or her. But for whatever reason, in that moment at the playground, my dad informed me that those words were not to be used in this manner. Jesus Christ was the son of God, and He could hear us all of the time. I didn't know exactly what he meant, but I learned not to use the Lord's name in vain, if nothing else. And that night when I climbed into bed with my sister, I said my first prayer and began to pray every night from then on. I prayed that if God was real and He could hear me that He would protect us and keep us safe, that He would have my mother return, and that He would help me to be the best little girl so that she would not need to leave again.

I gained many names from my childhood, but I also gained many fears—one was for safety. I wanted to be protected, to be held and known, and I longed for those things well into my adulthood. Even now, those are the themes and patterns that remain. Most of my chains can be followed right down into each of those names, and on your journey down you would find plenty of justifications strengthening each one.

You should know, I have searched most places to find the safety I long for: my marriage, my children, my health, my body, my friends, redeemed relationship with my mother, the death of my father—and each and every time I stumble into searching those places, they fail me. My husband will never be able to love me fully enough, my children are tiny terrorists out to destroy any feeling I hold that supports the idea that this mom thing is working out, my health fails daily in many ways—each movement brings pain and each pain reminds me that I can not heal myself. My body is also out of my control because of my health. My body's ability to be fit and active directly relies on my ability to be healthy. My friends have their own lives and needs and desires, and I fail them, and they fail me. The only hope in my relationship with my mother is the never-ending fountain of grace the Father provides for me to bestow upon her, which is still not enough for her. The death of my father remains a source of remorse and mourning over the loss of his life as well as the implications for my own story. Yet Jesus remains.

I have spent countless words through prayer asking God to convince me that I needed to experience any of the above. Asking Him why on earth He deemed me strong enough to withstand and hold those stories. Asking Him what His purpose was in any of it.

I have come to know and believe that safety lies within His knowledge of me. This safety that I have longed for through the majority of my life has not gone unseen or uncared for. This desire for understanding has been redeemed and caught up in a much larger story that He is still cultivating within me through His righteousness. What I spent a majority of my life seeing as evil He meant for good. And I have come to feel most safe when I rest in the knowledge that He has of me. The more fully known I believe that I am, the less I have to hide, the less I have to hold back. And the more willing I am to enter in despite my own understanding of belonging, the more I understand my need for redemption and the more I can openly confess. We are safe simply in the His knowledge of our very names. And what has become apparent to me, as well as hopeful, is the name He has for me belongs entirely to Him, and He is creating it out of His goodness and His truth and His sacrifice. He's creating this name out of the intimate knowledge He has of my story—not only in the beginning, from my creation—not just in my past, longing for redemption or healing—but also in my current weak standing and in my future need. He knows it all and still calls me His, and I don't believe it can get any safer than that.

In Isaiah 62:1–4, we read Isaiah's prayer for Jerusalem, in which he says that we will be given a new name by the Lord's own mouth. The Lord will hold us in His hand for all to see—a splendid crown in the hand of God. Never again will we be called "the forsaken city" or "the desolate land." Our new name will be "the city of God's delight" and "the Bride of God," for the Lord's delight is us, and he will claim us as His bride.

God is aware of your story and the names that have come from it. You are safe because He is not only aware of them but also currently and actively redeeming them and recreating them into something that is worthy of display in the palm of His very hand, a name that is worth delight and worthy of all He has to offer.

He not only died for your sins, so you could be washed entirely clean but also will return for your ultimate rescue in full awareness of the ugly names you have given yourself or been given by others and the stories that surround them. He is fully aware of your sin and shame and need for Him. And He is also aware of the times of rejoicing and the moments in which you have experienced and will experience restoration with Him. But all moments are the same in His eyes when you are with Him. You were worth it.

This truth is hope for the church, and that hope is what was meant for you. The idea of being renamed in His image is not only a source of safety but also a definition. No one is more aware of your story or your self-given names than the One who knit you together, the One whose Spirit dwells within you so you will never truly be alone, the One who will not only give you a new name but also cultivate it into beauty that reflects Him, the One who not only died to release you from your chains that bind but also will return for your ultimate and complete rescue from them. Sounds safe. Feels safe. Is safe. That's you.

Your safety has come through His intimate knowledge of your story—and not only that but also His knowledge of your very name. A name that you have already been given through His righteousness in light of your story as it has been caught up in His.

1. What are some of your self-given names?

2. Where did they come from?

Sounds safe. Feels safe. Is safe. That's you.

> Sing, O daughter of Zion;
> shout aloud, O Israel!
> Be glad and rejoice with all your heart,
> O daughter of Jerusalem!
>
> **—Zephaniah 3:14**

CHAINS

JESSICA K. JAGER

CHAINS

CHAINS

CHAPTER 4

TIME

Yet what we suffer now is nothing compared to the glory he will reveal to us later. For all creation is waiting eagerly for that future day when God will reveal who his children really are. Against its will, all creation was subjected to God's curse. But with eager hope, the creation looks forward to the day when it will join God's children in glorious freedom from death and decay. For we know that all creation has been groaning as in the pains of childbirth right up to the present time. And we believers also groan, even though we have the Holy Spirit within us as a foretaste of future glory, for we long for our bodies to be released from sin and suffering. We, too, wait with eager hope for the day when God will give us our full rights as his adopted children, including the new bodies he has promised us. We were given this hope when we were saved. (If we already have something, we don't need to hope for it. But if we look forward to something we don't yet have, we must wait patiently and confidently.)

And the Holy Spirit helps us in our weakness. For example, we don't know what God wants us to pray for. But the Holy Spirit prays for us with groanings that cannot be expressed in words. And the Father who knows all hearts knows what the Spirit is saying, for the Spirit pleads for us believers in harmony with God's own will. And we know that God causes everything to work together for the good of those who love God and are called according to his purpose for them. For God knew his people in advance, and he chose them to become like his Son, so that his Son would be the firstborn among many brothers and sisters. And having chosen them, he called them to come to him. And having called them, he gave them right standing with himself. And having given them right standing, he gave them his glory.

—Romans 8:18–30 NLT

Part of me wanted to share this message first. I wanted to give you the freedom to know that you didn't need to feel pressure to buy into any of this, that you could know there was nothing you had to actively and physically do to make any of this happen. I wanted to lead with this because I didn't want this series to become another chain, another thing that did the opposite of what it was intended to do. But I am seeing now— as I am literally soaking up the goodness of the simplicity and unbelievable freedom that this message is intended to bring— that the previous messages are what make this idea safe—not the other way around.

The idea of time can be freeing, but it can also be discouraging as we realize there is no quick fix for our depravity or need. That we can't simply make a choice for our hearts to be different, for our minds to be changed or our actions to be transformed, can be saddening as we come to know and believe that we weren't intended to be able to save ourselves. The reality is that all we can do is be available to the cultivating and propelling of the Spirit as He works and redeems and repairs our stories and our hearts. Our only role is wanting and waiting for and watching for Him. That reality can seem daunting. And through the reminder that our control was relinquished at the cross, I realized that without belief in the gospel and knowledge of our safety within it, the idea of time might actually not seem lovely.

The Bible tells us many things about time; we are given hope in it as well as freedom. I made a simple list of some of the words that are used in reference to it: forever, eternal, eternity, everlasting, with, constant, always, forevermore, never ending, endures, dwells, patient, steadfast, active, ages. Those words have had a way over the years of replacing my angst with a hopeful awareness of who He is and how He intends for me to experience Him as I long for full restoration with Him.

While preparing this message for the Restore women's gatherings, I had written something completely different, shared a completely different piece of my story, and in a way—I must confess—attempted to hide a piece of heart that I didn't know if I was strong enough to share. But through much prayer, encouragement from loved ones, more prayer, and some good old propelling of the Spirit, I was led to see that He wanted me to share my current groaning, not the stories of yesterday that, although worthy were cleaned up and packaged with a bow; they had answers and explanations. The story that He gave in replacement though is one of constant pursuit, one of longing, groaning, and wonder.

This story is not a hidden one; rather, I have shared it with those closest to me, I feel safe to share with those whom I know will not judge it, those who know my heart and His, those who know where I stand and where I long to be. Because they are the ones who know me apart from the pain. They are the people that know where my heart really lies and rests and waits. They are the people who know that I'm strong because of Him and I'm willing to wait for my ultimate healing because of Him. But today I will share with all of you who will listen and hear. Because I am safe in Him and the name He has for me, I will share with you about my deepest groaning: my health.

A year ago I was sitting in the kitchen of a dear friend surrounded by dear friends; I was sharing for the first time in complete openness about the daily struggle that is my life. You see, each day brings pain for me. Physical pain and suffering from the moment I wake, in fact for most of the moments that I sleep as well. I am constantly reminded that my body is broken, that my hips and spine do not have the ability to hold alignment, and that parts of my body are fused in a way that makes movement of any kind painful. I've had pain for ten years that ebbs and flows in severity but never leaves completely. I've done nothing short of trying to heal myself to make it stop, to prune my own tree, to outsmart or oversee my care. I've had tests that are uncountable at this point, imaging and blood and the like. I've tried naturopaths and diets and exercise routines, and ignoring the fact that I have a body that is beyond earthly repair and just demands management and attention. And in the last two years I have reached a new level of need, and my pain has been harder for me to contain. I don't share about it openly. That lack of sharing started as hiding and morphed into a desire for things to not be about me, which left me attempting to keep attention elsewhere, quietly dealing on the sidelines with what I had determined was a just my lot.

Back to the kitchen. My friend, my confidant, my heart holder, as I have deemed her, prays in what I could explain as an intercessory manner for what I could not pray: for my healing, for my ultimate healing and rescue and removal from the pain and suffering I experience. I wish I could say I loved that she did that, but really I felt as if we could be praying for more worthy things, things that were struggles or hardships for the others in that room, things that seemed more worth our breath and our time, because I was convinced that God wouldn't heal me, not couldn't just wouldn't. I had gotten to a point where I had equated my circumstance with what God had just determined me worthy to handle. I believed that He had deemed strong enough and my failure or inability was just proof that I couldn't handle my end of the deal. I'm sure this sounds similar to other stories I have shared; my chains are attached strongly here as well.

And so I will share with you the reality here—and what God has actually healed is nothing short of what I in fact needed Him to pay attention to. Every morning I wake and I pray that God will give me reminder of why I move. As I wake my babies, I am met with their earthly groaning as they are not removed from preteen and teen angst and "suffering." They are not welcoming of my entrance and invitation to rise for the day. And so I pray again that God will sustain me and not let me throw my pain at them, dousing their reality with mine, overshadowing what seems very real to them. And I climb the stairs again to return to the kitchen. With each step my hip grinds into my pelvis, clicking and popping the whole way. If it is a good day, sometime soon I will feel something clunk into place. With the clunk, I feel my heart rise to Jesus as I thank Him for a tiny mercy. This all falls within the first hour, and I have had to remain connected to him the whole way. It's not my favorite, and He knows that; I have to pray for much grace, and what He delivers is much mercy. And so we move forward.

The last two years have brought new realities and progression in my disease process. I have been at times under strict sanction of zero exercise. I have spent an inordinate amount of time attending pool parties for those at least forty years my senior, floating around and allowing people to manipulate my body into submission through physical therapy while feeling quite exposed and vulnerable in my bathing suit. I've heard many more nos than yeses in my interactions with health care professionals. I have been told that I should have picked different cards at the beginning of the game, that my hand is not one of hope. And in years past I would have agreed, but now it just angers me because that is the furthest thing from the truth that could be said about me. My body is not a liability to the mission or to the hope *He* has for me.

The morning of the day I preached on safety marked five weeks of taking a new medication to aid me in my psoriatic arthritis and ankylosing spondylitis. It was meant to help me with flares and pain. Along with it came a prescription for an anti-inflammatory that I have my friend Megan inject in my bottom weekly (it's a new level of community, I will have you know). With the new meds, I experienced five weeks of vomiting and diarrhea for twelve hours each day. The doctor had warned me that this was the common side effect and if I could hang in there it would pass, and so I quietly persevered. I hated it. It was awful. That morning, though, it was especially bad, and I reached out for prayer from those who surround me in this. It passed enough for me to preach, and then it returned the next morning, during which I ended up in urgent care. This required a lot of sacrifice for those around me, which is one of the things that make me the most uncomfortable. Brian was in Boise and couldn't help me, so I had to lean on my community—my family. This is what it required: someone took my kids to school, someone brought me Gatorade and started prompting me toward the urgent care, someone watched someone else's kids so they could take me in, others got off work early to take over childcare, Brian got an earlier flight home, and my friend Megan administered the care. I was never alone. In the past this would have brought sorrow; it would have brought shame. It would have felt defeating. In fact none of this would have even happened, as I would have taken myself in—and surely not to an urgent care where I might see someone I knew. But what God has used it for is love and healing. I did not necessarily love needing it, but He knew that and He provided me with mercy.

In the past couple years God's grace, forgiveness, and unmerited favor are some of the things I am much more aware of now than I have ever been in my life. But as of late there is another characteristic that relates to his compassion and kind and loving care for me even when I am undeserving. Mercy. I am always quick to believe that anything I am experiencing that resembles suffering in the least has been allowed for me to learn something from. I don't think that I believe God wants me to suffer as much as I believe that he has deemed it worthwhile. So praying for healing or asking for help out of painful or harsh situations seems invalid to me most of the time, as I believe there is always work to be done. I had a kind friend hear me explain this recently, and her response was full of the missing link: mercy. She told me what I was believing was simply not true and that, although she knew I would need to come to that realization on my own, God did not in fact want me to suffer, or feel pain. Although He can use it, pain is not part of his grace and mercy.

A summer ago, Brian and I set out with our kids on our annual family road trip. This is the stuff dreams are made of, folks. I knew, if nothing else, we would be met with an overwhelming awareness of our need for Him as we were met with angst, and fighting, probably some puke, and at least one threat of *don't make me pull this car over.* But nonetheless we do it year after year, because He's good to meet us in it, and we get to see His uninterrupted creation together and remember that He is not just Provider or Father or Forgiver but He is also Creator. This trip would take us to the beautiful dessert canyons of Utah to see as many national parks as we could in nine days. I knew this trip would bring hours in the car without being able to stretch, sleeping on hard ground, and movement—so much movement. And I knew all of this would equal pain, and a return trip home in much need of endless days trying to soak it off in the tub. I went through the first six days without pain, and on the sixth day we took a hike to a beautiful waterfall. The hike was nine miles round trip. With each step I took, I was in complete amazement, as I felt no pain, no discomfort, and I had energy to move forward with each mile. With each step, I learned more and more about Gods great mercy for me. It made no sense for my body to be without pain, for my lower spine to somewhat move and bend how it should (in a way that supported the rest of my body). And in a similar way, it was very confusing to take in the beauty surrounding me—my daughter Grace counted twenty different types of flowers, and there was a living stream full of fish, stone that stretched to the clouds on either side of the canyon as far as you could see, red sand at my feet, and the sound of birds and moving water—life in the desert. The closer we got to the waterfall, the more refreshing the air became, as it filled with a fresh mist and the air became a whole lot cooler than the triple digits we had experienced along the trail. And when we came around that last corner, my heart filled with awe and wonder as I reflected on this wonderful maker who not only made that waterfall in front of me but also made me and cares for it all in a way that is incomprehensible. I called a friend later that day to report of His goodness. But it wouldn't take long for my heart to falter, as we are fickle creatures and the next day was an experience much closer to what I thought I already knew.

The next day we hiked down into some of the most striking beauty I have ever seen. They were slot canyons, created by His wind that blows through the desert floor to make what almost appear as permanent waves in the sand. We must have hiked a half-mile down into the depths of these canyons, and a mile into the hike I began to realize that my dear sweet girl was not doing so well. You see, that girl is a human thermometer. If it's above 70 degrees you will be able to tell by the redness of her cheeks as her blood rises like mercury to her face with varying severity according to each change of the temperature above a balmy 70 degrees. Brian and I decided it would be best for her if we turned back and climbed out. He had seen a shortcut just a short ways back. The shortcut consisted of a steep, smooth climb up, but there were footholds along the way. Both the kids scampered up with very little difficulty followed by Brian and me holding up the rear. I got to about two feet from the top when I felt my hip release from the socket. It does this. It's like mild dislocation, and there is little I can do. I knew

I wasn't going any farther. I looked at Brian and said, *I can't.*
To which he replied, *I'll help you.* Fear took over, which was
quickly followed by anger, and I begged for them to leave me.
Brian wasn't going to be able to push me without harming
himself, and I was sure in my mom brain that my kids would
tumble to their death if they tried to come back down. And
so they did; they left me, and I hiked the mile back by myself,
the whole way yelling at God, angry and in lament—*yesterday
you delivered me pain free, but today you couldn't even give me
two feet. Why would you leave me here like this?* And I tell you,
friends, and not lightly, I heard Him speak to me, *I do not want
you here. You are not alone. I do not intend to leave you here. Get
out.* And I did, I got out. I climbed a craggy rocky hill crying
the whole way in complete awe of who he really is in contrast
with my own belief at times. We got back in our car, and I
weeped for the next four hours. I couldn't even explain what
was going on, but what had happened is that I had just had a
wrestling match with Jesus, and He won. I was not alone. I was
not the brokenness of my body. I was a daughter, captive in his
love and within his sight, and He did not intend to leave me in
that broken state to figure it out on my own.

Through this season has come a new way to pray: *God I have
no words, but I need you to heal me.* I'd love to tell you that
there has been miraculous healing in my spine—there has
not been. I'd love to tell you that I wake up everyday without
pain in my body—I do not. I'd love to tell you that I can do

CHAINS

all the things I long to do freely—I can't. But what I do know and what I can tell you is that I am held and it's okay for me to be broken. I find His mercy and grace most of all in the perfect mix of joy and sorrow that I experience in nearly every moment of my day, because without Him I am confident that even the joy would resemble sorrow. I am in pain through all of the things that bring me the most joy: when I pick up a baby, when I hug each of you, when I am with my husband, when I hike and run with my babies, and even when I sleep. But the pain is not where I rest anymore, and the diagnosis no longer holds my identity within it. I may never be healed earthside, but God has been good to heal my heart and my soul through the contentedness He has brought me in the simple awareness I have of His hand.

I believe that in the time He has us here, He plans to use each second, each part of our stories, to heal us, to free our hearts, to show us what it looks like to be loved, to be known, to be heard, and to be seen. And that's going to take some time, friends. It's going to take time for you to believe, but don't allow that to cause you to claw at your chains, trying to free yourself with every key you have, because it's already done. You're already free, and He's coming back.

That's why He came. He knew you would need a savior even before time began. He knew you would need His Spirit to be a constant supply of His heart and His goodness so that you could know that you had not been left alone. It's all already been provided, and you—in your simple and feeble belief—are already free.

There are many myths in the idea of the healing taking time. One is that healing stops and starts. It is a myth that in our stories it begins when we first believe and stops and stalls with each sin, each shortcoming, each moment of unbelief and begins again each time we believe in Him, see His goodness or believe His truth. The truth actually is that God has never once and never will take His eyes off of us—the sacrifice was meant to be continuous. It was finished when He died upon the cross, and our need to make ourselves good or right or worthy was torn to shreds and covered in His blood. And in that moment we were given an invitation to eternity where we will only receive His care and His goodness. And for now, while we wait for His return, we can wait in the knowledge of the Spirit He left with us so that we are never alone.

Your circumstance is rough. And it's hard. And most of it is probably only known by you, but, friend, He knows. And in that knowledge He has of our stories, we are not waiting for anything to begin—it has begun. We are not waiting to be ultimately healed—we have been healed. We are not waiting for an invitation into the family—we are the freaking family! And heaven, friends … it's worth longing for. The removal of earthly circumstance and worldly waiting—what freedom that will be. But we can claim it here in and through the knowledge He's given us. We can claim it by acting in the freedom made available to us through the gospel and our safety within it. Through the restoration of our vertical need with Christ we can enter into horizontal restoration with others, for it's our need that makes us more alike than different. We are loved and seen, and we were made with a need for community.

Know that your security is in heaven, yet God has left His Spirit here for you—and that while you wait for His return you are never alone. Knowing that His work is not for your happiness but for His purpose allows you to rest in His knowledge of your need and your suffering.

- **What is your earthly source of groaning?**

- **What about His glory has He left you with in order to comfort?**

Your groaning may be found in a story from your past before you were saved, in the present process of your restoration through Him, or in your hope for the future—within the ultimate promises of the completion of your salvation when you reach heaven's gates.

God intends to use your time here to heal you, to redeem your story, to free your heart, to show you what it looks like to be loved, to be known, to be seen, to be heard—and

that's going to take time. However, it is not intended to cause you to claw at your chains, driving you to try every key you can find to release yourself from your need in an attempt to free yourself from the result of your life in this broken world. Rather it is intended to allow you to feel the freedom you have been given, to fall at His feet, to rest in His hands that hold the keys for your ultimate release and rescue.

CHAINS

CHAINS

CHAINS

_____

_____

_____

_____

_____

_____

_____

_____

_____

_____

_____

_____

_____

_____

_____

_____

_____

_____

_____

_____

_____

_____

_____

_____

_____

_____

ENCOURAGEMENT TO DISCUSS CHAPTER QUESTIONS IN COMMUNITY

I am praying that as you read through this book you would take time to sift the contents of your heart through these questions. It is my hope and prayer that you would find some sisters to do that with, and that you would feel safe enough in the knowledge He has of you to be vulnerable and honest and open to those sisters. One of the most beautiful things about my own story of restoration has been that He has never once left me alone in my desire for closeness with Him. Being true to what He has intended for me in community, He has provided me with ladies to walk by me through much of it. This has healed my story and my heart in many ways, but most significantly, it has restored my view of family and community. We were meant to experience life together, and that life is, at the root, found within His hands. I have great hope for our restored relationship with Him, and it is my continued prayer that His blessing would allow us to have a renewed experience of sisterhood within that.

As I preached these messages in a room filled mostly with women who aren't only my friends but my dear and precious family, I was reminded that He hears, He knows, and He loves—and He desires for us to be near Him. And He will not stop short of anything to see that plan through. As I lay in my parents' backyard almost a year and half ago, praying that He would reveal His plan for me, He gave me a vision for all of you. There were seven faces shown to me in my living room, and I recognized each one. I remember asking Him what He wanted, doubting what He had shown me. And the biggest reason for my doubt was that I knew the stories held in the hearts belonging to those faces. I knew those stories held hurt with one another and that the looks on their faces did not match their current ability to relate with one another. From what I understood, there wasn't a way for those women to sit with one another in a way that would reflect hope, that would reflect longing for one another's hearts and rejoicing for one another's joy. What He was showing me was the impossible, but what He had in mind was nothing short of a miracle. I started praying, asking Him to show me what He had, and what He revealed is that we needed to experience restoration in Him before we could experience restoration with one another. And what was born out of that was a dream for Restore Gatherings: time for women to delve into the gospel in the search for freedom, for hope and for peace in Him, time to experience restoration together.

When I walked into the space we used for the Restore Gatherings the first night, I saw chairs filled with the seven bottoms He had shown me in that vision joined by eighty other women longing to know more of Him. I was nearly unable to speak, as I have never experienced His love and provision in such a way. As I shared His words, I was struck by a wave of humbleness as I was given the privilege of seeing how those words met a lot of those women personally because of the knowledge He had already given me of their stories. I felt trepidation in knowing that He was not giving me a message of more to do or of shame but a message of freedom, of restoration, and of life: the gospel. And furthermore, I not only knew that message but also believed it and so desperately needed it myself.

The months leading up to these gatherings, and even the time of preaching, were full of much restoration for myself, as I had to continually return to His throne for the strength to continue, the perseverance to continually hope, and the weakness to let go of the whole thing and let Him move in the way He intended to move. I believe He used that time to strengthen my own testimony as well as to secure for me a stronger knowledge of who He really is and what He has come to do.

I know very little of the days to come, but I know that I have been called to be a proclaimer of hope, a preacher of the good news, a teacher of His word, and a recorder of His testament within me. And through that, I will continually and humbly approach His throne asking for what's next.

Printed in the United States
By Bookmasters